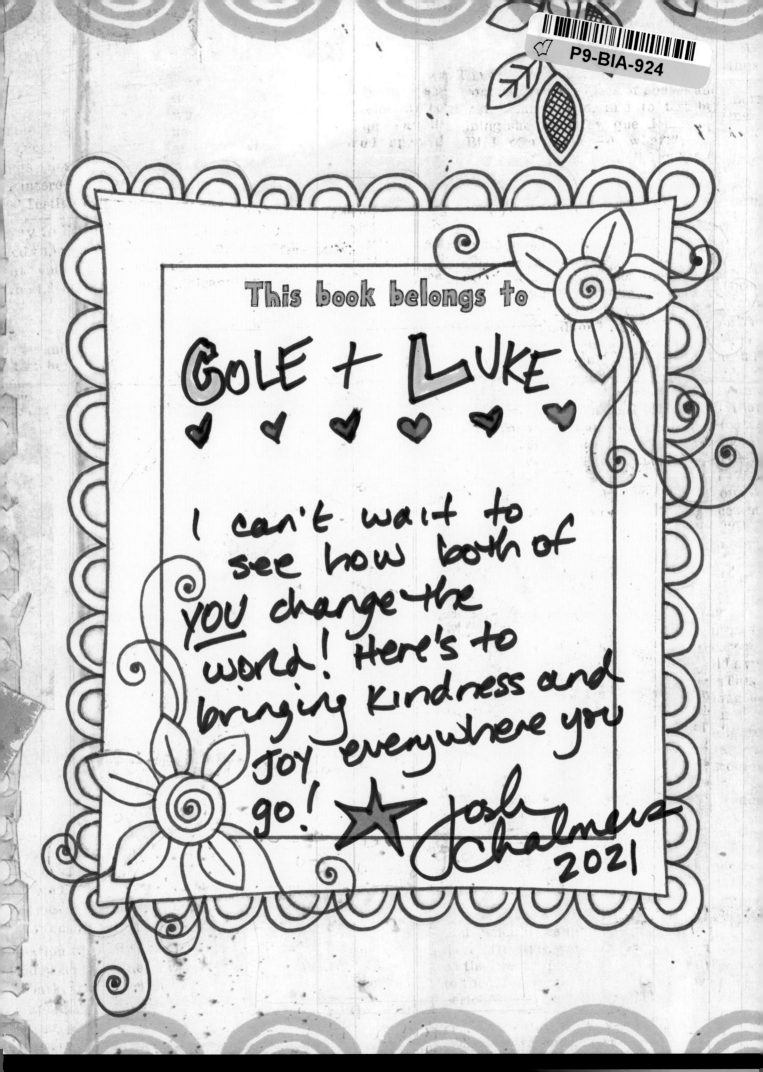

This book belongs to

COLE + LUKE

I can't wait to see how both of YOU change the world! Here's to bringing kindness and joy everywhere you go! ⭐ Josh Chalmers 2021

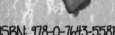
Published by Schiffer Publishing, Ltd.
4880 Lower Valley Road
Atglen, PA 19310
Phone: (610) 593-1777; Fax: (610) 593-2002
E-mail: Info@schifferbooks.com
Web: www.schifferbooks.com

For our complete selection of fine books on this and related subjects, please visit our website at www.schifferbooks.com. You may also write for a free catalog.

Schiffer Publishing's titles are available at special discounts for bulk purchases for sales promotions or premiums. Special editions, including personalized covers, corporate imprints, and excerpts, can be created in large quantities for special needs. For more information, contact the publisher.

We are always looking for people to write books on new and related subjects. If you have an idea for a book, please contact us at proposals@schifferbooks.com.

Other Schiffer Books on Related Subjects:
Zendoodle for Children by Gitta Edelmann, ISBN: 978-0-7643-5413-7
The Cycling Wangdoos by Kelly Pulley, ISBN: 978-0-7643-5406-9

CHANGE THE WORLD BEFORE BEDTIME

Illustrated by
KAREN GOOD

MARK Kimball moulton

Josh Chalmers

A collaboration by three big dreamers

Schiffer Publishing Ltd

4880 Lower Valley Road • Atglen, PA 19310

Change the world before bedtime.
It's easy. You'll see!
Sharing a part of your heart is the key.

So leap out of bed, tie your hero cape on,
Let's show our true colors before the day's gone.

We'll eat a good breakfast of fruit and whole grains-
we need super foods for our bodies and brains.

Then we'll soar through the day doing random good deeds, turning frowns upside down with spectabulous speed.

And with each super deed, we'll grow faster and stronger. As more heroes join us, the "good deeds list" grows longer (and longer and longer)!

We might know of someone who's lonely or sick.
We'll visit with cupcakes and give them first pick!

Or maybe we'll gather warm clothing and toys
to help some less fortunate girls and boys.

1.00

Donations

HeLp us
♥ buiLd ♥
a weLL
in Uganda.

Or perhaps, as a group, we'll sell cold lemonade,
along with fresh cookies and crafts that we've made.
Then we'll donate our time and the money we've raised
to a school overseas. They'll be simply amazed!

We'll be kind to the Earth, we'll conserve, save a frog;
Recycle, bicycle, hug a tree, pet a dog.

We'll think happy thoughts and we'll say happy words—
The happiest words that the world ever heard.

And later, we'll join all our friends for some fun,
to share in the goodness our good deeds have done.

Folks will ask, "What's your secret? What gives you such powers?
You've made the world better in just a few hours!"
And we'll say, "Just believe. You can be super, too!
Start small and think big and you'll make dreams come true."

No matter the season, we'll do what we can
to brighten the spirit of our fellow man.

There'll be laughter and flowers and rainbows above,
'cause happy things happen when hearts shine with love.

You'll see hero capes flying in colorful hues,
purples and pinks and bright reds and blues!
Each cape will be different, and yet much the same,
you get to choose what your cape will proclaim!

So dream your own dreams in your own special way.
Put cheerful, kind thoughts in the things that you say.
Be caring to others and take time to play.

And we'll all change the world by the end of the day!

GOOD DEEDS TO DO IDEAS PAGE

NOTES

DATE

HAPPY WORDS FROM AROUND THE WORLD

Bien Fait!
Well done!
in French

Scusa
Excuse me.
in Italian

CU PLACERE!
You're welcome!
in Romanian

GRACIAS!
Thank you!
in Spanish

nĭ zhēn bàng!
You're awesome!
in Chinese

Hezky den.
Have a nice day.
in Czech

HEBU KUWA MARAFIKI.
Let's be friends.
in Swahili

Mwen kapab fe pou ou.
I can help you.
in Haitian Creole

het is een mooie dag
It's a beautiful day.
in Dutch

VOCE E FANTASTICO!
You're fantastic!
in Portuguese

B'hatzlachah
Good luck! in Hebrew

volim te
I love you
in Croatian

MAKE YOUR OWN SUPERHERO CAPE

Start with A pillowCASE.

X ← X
cuT HOLES and tiE On Ribbons

↓ opening on bottom ↓

LUCY

SAVE THE WHALES!

Then add YOuR namE AnD SPeciAL dEcoRations.

Ta-DA!

SPeciaL Instructions

SUPPLY LiST
- ☐ PiLLowGASE
- ☐ fAbric MarKERS
- ☐ stickERS
- ☐ sAFeTy Scissors
- ☐ iRon-on LETTERS
- ☐ GLuE STiCK
- ☐ 2 long ribbonS
- ☐ strEamerS
- ☐ ------------
- ☐ ------------

CTWBB

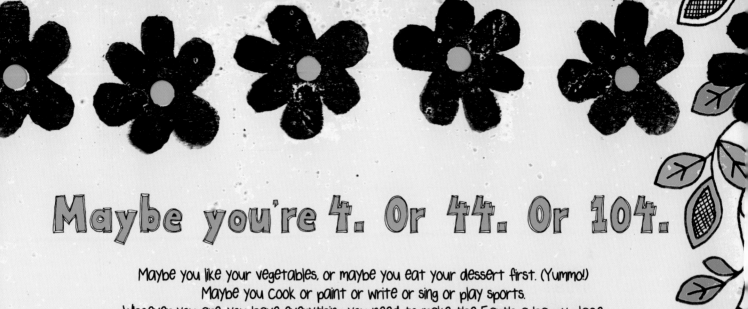

Maybe you're 4. Or 44. Or 104.

Maybe you like your vegetables, or maybe you eat your dessert first. (Yummo!)
Maybe you cook or paint or write or sing or play sports.
Whoever you are, you have everything you need to make the Earth a happy place.
Your heart, your brain, your kindness, your friendship, your big dreams—these are your superpowers.
One day, maybe you'll use them to CHANGE THE WORLD.
So get out your hero cape . . .
Maybe that day is
TODAY.

A FEW PROJECTS FOR COLLABORATION, ADULTS WELCOME!

Host a Neighborhood Fundraiser

1) Choose a nonprofit organization you'd like to help.

2) Decide what type of neighborhood fundraiser you'd like to host. A lemonade stand or craft sale are great ideas!

3) Get organized. Think about what you'll need and gather your materials. Make a list and check it twice. (Perhaps thrice!)

4) Find the perfect location. It needs to be safe, but also busy, so you'll have lots of happy customers.

5) Get creative! Use your "inner artist" to make big, happy signs to let folks know what you're planning. Include the date, time, and location on these signs.

6) Post your signs on bulletin boards at school, at your local library, and in neighborhood stores, but always ask permission first.

7) The morning of the event, jump out of bed early and eat a good breakfast. There's lots of fun to be had! Decorate your table and the surrounding area. Wear your hero cape and ask your helper-heroes to wear theirs, too. Nothing will be better for promoting sales! Display more of those amazing signs to let folks know what a wonderful thing you're doing for our world.

8) Keep your sale items clean and fresh-looking throughout the day.

9) Keep careful track of your sales with the help of an adult.

10) At the end of the day, clean up and leave the area as you found it. Recycle as much waste as possible. Properly dispose of everything else. Only happy memories of your event should remain.

11) Finally, donate the money you make to your chosen nonprofit and—abracadabra—you've helped to Change the World Before Bedtime! The only thing left to do is to get a good night's sleep, knowing you are a true hero, indeed.

Help Your Local Food Pantry

Sadly, there are people all over our world who go to bed hungry every day. Sometimes they live in our very own neighborhoods. Fortunately, anti-hunger organizations do their best to help, but they, in turn, need you. Ask your local food pantry what items they REALLY need. They're always happy to supply a list of these items. Then, organize a food drive. Ask your friends, family, and other kindhearted folks to donate items from the list. After you collect the supplies, deliver them to the pantry. You'll be greeted by happy smiles and happy words, and our big, beautiful world will thank you. Who knows? Maybe you'll discover you'd like to get more involved and become a volunteer. And maybe, sometime in the future, there won't be a need for food pantries anymore and everyone around the world will go to bed with enough food in their bellies. What a wonderful day that would be!

Support Clean Water Projects

Wouldn't it be incredible to help people who don't have access to clean water? We are truly fortunate to enjoy safe water in our homes and schools, but this isn't the case in many parts of our world, or even in some parts of our own country. You can use the same helpful hints from our other ideas to host a fundraising event to bring solutions to this problem. Perhaps you might host a fundraising breakfast (who doesn't love pancakes?) or an art show or a bake sale in partnership with your school. Put your thinking cap on. Just imagine—you'll actually help to save lives!

Donate New Or Gently Used Clothing, Books, And Toys

Nearly every community has a place that accepts the gently used clothes, books, and toys (including bikes and sports equipment) that you've outgrown. They donate these items to folks who will love them and put them to good use. Ask your family, school groups, civic organizations, and, of course, all your hero-friends to box up their goods and bring them to those donation outlets. You'll bring joy and comfort to so many people at the same time. Hearts will grow and smiles will shine, and the world will be a better place.

What You Can Do in Your Very Own Community

There's nothing better than volunteering. You'll meet so many talented, interesting people. You'll make new friends and change the world at the same time. You and your family can volunteer at schools, community events, holiday parades, sporting events, fundraising concerts, walk-a-thons, animal adoption days—the list goes on and on.

What You Can Do to Help Change the Whole, Wide, Wonderful World

Think global! It's important that we all gain a better understanding of the way people in other countries live—what they believe in, how they grow up, what makes them happy and healthy—and what they need to make their lives the very best they can be. Ask your teachers, parents, grandparents, and caregivers to help you learn more about our world and how it works. Get introduced to diverse books that share stories about kids across the planet, visit galleries and museums with international art exhibits, try new foods from other countries, and dig in to craft and creative projects that have their roots in cultures from around the globe. You'll soon discover that, despite our differences, we share similarities, too. Everyone around the world has hopes and dreams. The more we know, the more we're able to help each other make those hopes and dreams come true! And the faster we can Change The World Before Bedtime.

Hasn't this been fun? But there's so much more that can be done.
You'll find more information, resources, creative ideas, success stories,
big dreamer profiles, and inspiration here:
www.changetheworldbeforebedtime.com.